1985p

gr. 2-4

DATE DUE

FEB 2004	
DEC 2006	
OCT 2008	

DEMCO, INC. 38-2931

A DAY IN THE LIFE OF A
High-Iron Worker

by John Harding Martin
Photography by Gayle Jann

Troll Associates

Library of Congress Cataloging in Publication Data

Martin, John Harding.
    A day in the life of a high-iron worker.

    Summary: Follows a high-iron construction worker
through his day as he skillfully bolts together the iron
frame of a skyscraper.
    1. Building, Iron and steel—Vocational guidance—
Juvenile literature. 2. Construction industry—Vocational
guidance—Juvenile literature.   3. Cameron, Robert.
[1. Structural steel workers. 2. Occupations.
3. Cameron, Robert] I. Jann, Gayle, ill.   II. Title.
TH1615.M37   1985   693'.71   84-2449
ISBN 0-8167-0107-5 (lib. bdg.)
ISBN 0-8167-0108-3 (pbk.)

Robert Cameron's day begins at quarter to five in the morning. In his job as a high-iron construction worker, he helps put together the frames for tall buildings. His current job site is a big-city sky-scraper. The train gets him into the city in time to get to the construction site by eight o'clock.

3

He makes it to the construction site around quarter to eight. Before work begins, Robert must change into his work clothes in a trailer on the unfinished second floor of the building. The project he is working on will one day be a luxury hotel.

As the workday begins, Robert gets his equipment in order. He wears his wrenches on a utility belt. He also carries two very heavy pieces of equipment—a "pneumatic gun," used to tighten bolts, and a "power vane," which can enlarge the holes into which the bolts must fit.

To get to where he will be working for the day, Robert must climb up a series of ladders. He carries his heavy equipment with him. As work on the building progresses and the structure rises higher, temporary elevators will be installed to make his trip quicker and easier.

The most dangerous part of high-iron work is walking along the exposed steel girders. Robert can now do this easily and naturally, but it wasn't that way at first. He didn't learn how to do it overnight, either. He has been a high-iron worker for seven years.

It takes special skills to be able to move around on girders and work high above the street. Robert was a versatile athlete in high school, so he has the agility he needs to do his job well. But agility alone is not enough. Robert must also be constantly alert.

While he works, Robert often stands on a small platform that hangs from the girder. This platform is called a "float." The float gets Robert closer to the bolts he must tighten, and it gives him a good angle to work from.

The safety net under Robert's work station offers some protection in case he should fall. The net is similar to those used in circuses by trapeze artists and tightrope walkers. Robert's job will never be free of danger, but safety precautions can reduce the chance of serious injury.

Robert's main job is to tighten the bolts that hold the frame of the building together securely. He uses a powerful pneumatic gun for this. The gun vibrates so much that Robert must be sure he is steady and well braced when he uses it.

Sometimes a bolt does not fit properly into its hole. Then Robert uses his power vane to enlarge the holes in the girders. The power vane has a tendency to "kick," so using it can be dangerous. That's why Robert often asks for help when he uses this tool.

Bolts are too heavy for ironworkers to carry around in large quantities, so Robert works with only a few at a time. When he runs out of bolts, he calls down to a lower level, where a large supply of bolts is stored. Other workers place the bolts in a bucket, which is then hoisted up on a pulley.

Another worker, the "plumber-up," checks Robert's completed work. The plumber-up's job is to make sure that the building goes up straight. He twists a "turnbuckle," which tightens cables attached to two steel girders. The cables pull on the girders, slowly moving them until they are straight.

Whenever Robert works near the edge of the building, where there is no safety net, he is required to protect himself with a safety line. The rope that he uses ties to his belt and is looped through a bolt hole in the nearest piece of steel.

Robert breaks for lunch around eleven-thirty. It is a very hot day, and everyone has been working steadily, so a break is welcome. Robert joins a co-worker on top of a large steel girder. The huge crane needed to construct the building rises up behind them.

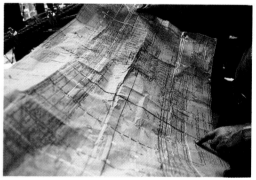

Before returning to work, Robert stops at ground level to consult with the foreman. Briefly, they go over the blueprints—the plans for the building. Usually, Robert knows what to do without asking, but he likes to check in with the foreman from time to time.

Back on the job, Robert uses a torch that will soften the steel around a particularly difficult hole. This allows him to get a bolt in place when the power vane is not able to make the hole large enough. Robert wears protective goggles when he uses the torch.

Meanwhile, down on the street, some of Robert's coworkers hook the cable of the crane to a huge steel column. This particular column weighs twenty-six tons! The crane hoists the column up to the highest level of the building, where other workers are waiting for it.

Now the crane slowly lowers the column so the "connectors" can guide it into place. These workers must position the steel so that "bolters" like Robert can do their job. Moving a piece of steel the size of this column is very dangerous and must be done with great care.

After Robert finishes tightening the bolts, the welder seals the connection between the steel girders. Using an electric arc, the welder melts a metal rod along the joint where steel meets steel. Robert often gives the welder a hand.

Sometimes, a joint that has already been welded is found to be slightly out of alignment. Another welder—one who uses a carbon arc—must undo the sealed joint. The sparks really fly when this has to be done. An air line attached to the carbon arc blows the molten metal away from the joints.

Robert often takes time out to explain different aspects of the work to young apprentices. Apprentices in high-iron construction work need a lot of encouragement, yet they must also learn to be patient. It takes time to get used to such demanding and dangerous work.

While learning about high-iron work, an apprentice is expected to do a wide variety of jobs. These tasks help the experienced workers get the more difficult work done. One of the apprentice's tasks is to carry blueprints to different parts of the building so that the workers can refer to them when necessary.

The "surveyor" has the final responsibility for making sure that the building goes up straight. Trained in mathematics, he must be certain that each portion of the building is precisely aligned. He checks constantly to see that girders have been cast properly at the foundry where they were made.

A few times a week, more steel is delivered to the construction site aboard flatbed trucks. With the help of the crane, workers quickly unload the steel. Then the crane lifts the steel from street level to the floor where it will be used.

As the building grows higher, the lower floors are covered with "decking"—corrugated metal laid down over the girders. Workers can now walk from place to place more easily than when they had to walk along the girders themselves. The decking also reduces the chance of accidents.

Now Robert tightens the last bolt of the day. High-iron construction calls for hard physical labor, and Robert is tired at the end of the day. He starts down the ladder, but before he leaves the building he will make one last stop.

A quick stroll out onto the crane gives Robert the opportunity to look over the progress that's been made on the building that day. Sometimes it seems as if things progress very slowly. But at other times Robert is amazed at how fast the huge pieces of steel rise up.

After changing into his street clothes, Robert makes his way to the top of a nearby building. From this vantage point, he can see the round central tower of the building he is working on. Surrounding the tower is the decking of the lower floors, plus the framework he has just bolted together.

In the evenings, Robert often works at a different kind of construction—small projects he can complete by himself. Tonight he is working on a coffee table made out of scrap materials from the skyscraper he's helping to build in the city.

At home, away from the city and its skyscrapers, Robert thinks about all the things that make his job a rewarding and satisfying one. Alone, high above the busy city streets, a high-iron construction worker is close to being "on top of the world."